Bl
Dl

C000205287

A selection of words and anecdotes
from around Bristol

by
Louise Maskill

BRADWELL
BOOKS

Published by Bradwell Books
9 Orgreave Close Sheffield S13 9NP
Email: books@bradwellbooks.co.uk

British Library Cataloguing in Publication Data:
a catalogue record for this book is available from the
British Library.

1st Edition

ISBN: 9781909914230

Print: Gomer Press, Llandysul, Ceredigion SA44 4JL

Artwork and design by: Andrew Caffrey

Photograph Credits: Shutterstock, iStock,
www.pastandpresentpublications.com
and Creative Commons

BRISTOL DIALECT

by Louise Maskill

ACKNOWLEDGEMENTS

This book came together at the request and with the support of Chris Gilbert; I am indebted to him for photographs, encouragement and the occasional kick in the pants. Tom, Molly, Owen and Caitlin have encouraged me throughout and made their own contributions to the A-to-Z, and have also provided a good deal of moral support. Tom also found errors aplenty in early drafts; any that remain in the book are my responsibility, not his.

Huge thanks to all of you.

DEDICATION

For Molly, Owen and Caitlin

Ef good thengs ye get noo lack o'
And ye feels tir'd out or lazy,
Light yer pipe, and blaw yer 'bacco,
Take et yazy.

Agrikler

Introduction

Although dialects are still evident in everyday speech from different parts of the country, they are nowhere near as common or as diverse as they used to be. This gradual extinction has been noted and mourned by writers and antiquarians over many years, and huge efforts have been made to capture the colloquial speech of men and women from various parts of the country.

Bristol, the unofficial capital city of the South West of England, has a warm-toned and sing-song dialect with distinct influences from the local Somerset and Gloucestershire dialects, but which has also been influenced by Welsh, Cornish and by maritime visitors down the centuries; Bristol has always been a major trading port, and as with other maritime cities, incoming speech patterns have left their mark in the local dialect. The speech of the city is known for the length of its vowels, the Bristol L and the sometimes confusing interchange of tenses and pronouns, but above all it is a friendly and welcoming dialect, to match the city and its people.

The first part of this book is an A to Z of words and phrases arranged with their meanings and a few examples of usage, while the second part contains a collection of anecdotes, stories, rhymes and curiosities, all arranged by theme. Some of the words in the A to Z are now in common use in everyday English, but the aim is to indicate their provenance in the old Bristol dialect. The anecdotes may be long or short, complicated or simple, but all contain genuine examples of Bristol dialect as gathered by myself or recorded by historians and collectors over the years.

Pointing the way to Bristol Shutterstock/Pontus Edenberg

Glossary

A

A – of, to or the

Aarsh – harsh

Ackrut, ackrutlee – accurate, accurately

Aeriawl – area or region

What aeriawl do ee live in?

Alligator's back – a local name for the serrated ridge of roof tiles which run the length of a tiled roof

Ambag – handbag

Amblance – ambulance

Amt – have not

Ancient – a West Country, and particularly Bristolian, term for the Union Flag of the British Isles when it is flown from a seagoing vessel

Ow can anyon tell when her is, if her ont show her ancient?

Ank – to go fast, sometimes without regard to safety

Blige! Ee anked it roun that corner, mind!

Ankle strap – a name for a particular type of child's shoe, like a slipper but with an ankle strap to keep in on

Anneye – haven't I

Annus – haven't we

Ansum – handsome. Often used as a term of endearment or as part of a greeting

Awlrite, me ansum?

Ant – has not

Anudder – another

Giv I anudder, willee?

Ar – our

Ark – listen to me

Assant – haven't or hasn't

Ast – ask

At – had

Ater – after

Av – have

Avs – has

Awd – old

Awlful – awful

Awlrite – alright. Often used as a general purpose greeting (see *ansum* above)

B

Babby, babber – baby, or sometimes used as a word for friend

Back – a strip of wharfage on the dockside, from a quarter to half a mile in length

Backee – to give someone a ride on the crossbar or handlebars of a bike

Badger – a dealer in corn

Baff – Bath, a city south east of Bristol

Baity – annoyed, cross

Ee was getten right baity.

Bammington – the game of badminton

Basdurd – bastard

Beamer – a blush caused by embarrassment

Look at the gurt beamer on ee!

Benny – rage or tantrum. To have a benny is to lose one's temper

Bide – remain, as in bide still

Bin – been

Bis/bist – are you. Often used as part of a greeting

Ow bist?

Bissen – is not

Blad – idiot, foolish person

Blige – goodness me! Good heavens!

Borrawl – borrow

Brindsey – brown or brindled, as of a dog's coat

Brung – brought

Burton – a type of cheap blended beer drunk by the poor in Bristol

When the Burton came we found that it was a very poor drink – a sort of small beer.

Buzzer – a bumble bee

The Avon gorge and the Clifton Suspension Bridge

Shutterstock/ariadna de raadt

C

Cacks – underwear

Camrawl – camera

Canave – can I have

Canave one a they?

Cas – can

Casn't – can't

Caw – coal

Cawd – cold

Chessaroon – a name for a poisonous kind of fungus, once found in abundance around Portishead

Chimley – chimney

Churz – cheers, thank you!

Cocker – friend

Come tight – to be painful or hurt

Coopie – crouch, as in *coopie down*, crouch down

Cudda – could have

D

Dap – run

Dapper – a small child

Daps – running shoes or plimsolls

You needs yer daps to do PE.

Das or dats – that is

Dedder or deddun – a corpse

Dill – deal

Dinnum – didn't they

Dint – did not

Discolated – dislocated

Disn't – did not

Dissis – this is

Doggin up – to glare threateningly

Yer, ee's doggin I up.

Dohnee – doesn't he

Do – to manage, to get on and flourish

My pigs do do very well by this new meal.

Dollop – a lump or quantity of something

Done – did

Draw – a sledge, commonly used to haul wheat or fallen trees on farms

Drawlen – a drawing or illustration

Dreckly – directly, straight away

Drive – affectionate term for a bus driver, used when alighting, as in *Cheers, drive!*

Drived – drove

Dunnee – doesn't he

Dunt – doesn't

Dursn't – dare not

E

Eda – he does
Ee – he, him, this, that, it
Eeuz – he was
Eeve – he has
Elemm – eleven
Er – or
Erd – heard
Evsa – ever so
Eyar – here you are

F

Falled – fell
Famlay – family
Fanks – thank you
Fer – for
Feud – if you had
Fin – thin
Fine – find
Fink – think
Fire up – to beat up or thrash
Ford – afford
Forn – an abbreviation of Blackthorn, a common variety of cider

Mine's a pint o' forn.

The Clifton Suspension Bridge Shutterstock/Alan Kraft

Founderous – a word used to describe Bristol's muddy roads

Free – three

Frim – for him

Frizz – for his

Frumety or frumenty – a warm drink made of boiled wheat, strained, sweetened and spiced, which was once sold at Bristol market

Fry – for me

G

Gabbart – a sailing vessel for inland navigation that used to ply the Avon upstream of Bristol

Gas – Bristol Rovers Football Club

Gashead – a supporter of Bristol Rovers

Gawf – the game of golf

Gawld – gold

Gehoe – a type of farm vehicle, a sledge without wheels dragged by horses

Gibbim – give him or gave him

Gif I it or giss – please give that to me

Glider – cider

Goa – go to

Gob or gobbed – spit or spat

Goes – going

Gonna – going to

Gout or goute – an underground passage for water

Grampfer – grandfather

Grampfer Grey – a woodlouse

Jew see the size a that Grampfer Grey?

Granner – grandmother

Guddun – a good one

Guff – to break wind

Gurt – great, large, very

Gwahn, gwahn en – go on, go on then

H

Haemony – the Bristolian name for the lemon-scented agrimony plant

Hardun – usually a young person with an attitude

Hobbler – a man who goes out to sea to meet homeward-bound vessels and guide them into harbour

*Note: this section is short, because it is said that no true Bristolian ever pronounces an **H** at the start of a word!*

I

I – I have, or me

Ideawl – an idea

Ijut – an idiot

SS Great Britain in Bristol Docks
Shutterstock/Jon Le-Bon

Ill – a hill

Im – him

Inchew – aren't you

Innit – isn't it

Innum – isn't it, isn't he/she or aren't they

Int – is not, am not

Is – his

Ise – I am

Iss – it is

J

Jammer – someone who is very lucky

Jammy – lucky

Jan – a tramp

Jasper – a wasp

Jeerme – did you hear me?

Jestabout – very much so

Jew – did you, do you

Jib – the mouth

Jitter – a person (particularly a male) with long hair

K

Keener – a degoratory term for someone who works hard

Kiddie – boy or youth (slightly derogatory)

Kinave – can I have

L

Laff – laugh

Laters – see you later

Lav – I will have

Lav one a they, fanks.

Laver – the edible seaweed which grows up the west coast of Britain, once relied on as a foodstuff by the poor fisher-folk of the Bristol Channel

Lease – least

Led – to lie down (past tense)

A bin led down all day.

Leevellen – evening

Lend – borrow

Lent – borrowed

Lessaf – can I have

Lesson – less than

Like – useful all-purpose word often added to the end or middle of sentences. At the end, it adds emphasis. In the middle, it substitutes for erm or ah

Look – another useful work, added to sentences for emphasis or to draw the listener's attention to something

Lush – nice, good, desirable

Luvver – mate, pal, dear, as in *alright, my luvver?*

M

Macky – very big

Marnin or marnen – morning

Mawday – mouldy

They cakes is all mawday!

Mazen – amazing

Me – my

Member – to remember

Mentalist – psychopath, nutter, mad person

Meself – myself

Mind – useful all-purpose word added to the beginning or end of sentences for emphasis. Means something like you know what I mean?

Mint – very good

Moran – more than

Muh – mother

Munf – month

Munt, munter – unattractive, not very nice

N

Nebbersin – never seen

Needaws – needles

Neever – neither

Nerr – never

You dint win? Nerr mind.

Nickies – bundles of thorns or hedge prunings
No – not
Nurlay – nearly

O

Of – have
Off of – off
Oh ah – I understand
Ohm – home
Oo – who
Ooze – who is
Oozee – who is he, who does he
  Ark at ee, oozee fink ee is?
Osbidal – hospital
Outride – a commercial traveller

P

Pacifically – specifically
Pataytawls – potatoes
Painen – in pain, hurting
  Ass painen I rotten.
Peepaw – people
Pikelet – crumpets

Clifton Suspension Bridge
Shutterstock/Antonio Abrignani

Pill – a fishing village on the coast with a creek or stream

Pirates – another name for the Bristol Rovers
Football Club

Pitch – to send to market

> *There idn a quarter so much wool a-pitched to Bristol Fair*
> *as used to.*

Pitchen – settling

> *Look, the snow's pitchen outside!*

Pitcher – picture

Pown – pound

Praps – perhaps

Proper – good, decent

Puddies – hands

Q

Quicken – a fast one

R

Raggy – a hand-rolled cigarette

> *Wan a raggy?*

Rawl – a bread roll

Razbrizz – raspberries

Rit – wrote

Robins – a name for Bristol City Football Club

Rown – around

Rus – or else

S

Sabout – it's about

Sarternun – this afternoon

Saint – this isn't

Sawd – sold

Scaw – school

Scowen – are you going?

Scrage – a small graze

A fell over an scraged me knee – got a macky scud, see?

Scrumps – small pieces of fried batter; a great fish-and-chip shop delicacy

Scud – a scab (often the consequence of a scrage)

Scutler – a promiscuous girl, or else Lambert and Butler cigarettes

See – useful word added to the end of sentences to emphasise meaning or ask for agreement

Seegaw – a seagull

Seen – saw

Seenin – saw him

Semm – seven

Shag – a friend, a mate

Shot away – mad or insane

The Victoria Rooms, now part of the University of Bristol

Shrammed – freezing, shivering with cold

Shup – shut up

Sleever – a straight pint glass

Slider – a playground slide

Smooth – to stroke, as in *smoothen the cat*

Smornen – this morning

Spanner – an idiot

Spinner – a liar

Spooner – someone who is not overly bright

Spoony – uncool

Spreethed – skin that is rough and cracked because of cold weather

Stingers – stinging nettles

Sunner – old friend, old mate (male)

Swellead – arrogant self-satisfied person

T

Ta – to

Taint – it isn't

Tamorra – tomorrow

Tawd – told

Thas – that is

Thee – you

Theirselves – themselves

Them – those

They's or they'm – they are

Tight – mean, miserly

Tis – it is

To – from, when used as a reference to a location

Where's that to?

Toon – to him

Toppers – the crusty end slices of a loaf of bread

Trow – a two-masted sea-going trading vessel, once common around the Bristol coast

Truss – a large bundle of hay

Tub or tub-fish – the gurnard

Tump – a small grassy hill

Twas – it was

Twat – to hit or bash

U

Uddent, ussent or unt – wouldn't

Ullee – will you

Un – one, or he

Unket – lonely or unsafe, as in an unket road

Up – to

V

Vawlse – a vase

Vench – adventure playground
Virrickawl – vehicle

W

Wallop – a hit or thump
Was/were – were/was
> *These two terms are used in the opposite way as in RP English.*
> *We was over there; ee were proper poorly.*

Wassat – what's that
Wayten – waiting
Weeda – we do
Weem – we are
Wernit – wasn't it
Whas – what is
Where's – where are, where is
Wig – a plain halfpenny bun sold by the bakers of Bristol and bought as a treat for children
Wunt – was not

X, Y, Z

Yawl – you will
Yeeren – hearing
Yer – hey, excuse me; or here
> *Yer, you seen ar littlun?*

Ah, ee's over yer.

Yers – ears

Yeserday – yesterday

Yewar – here you are

Yourn – yours

Zackly – exactly

Zat – is that

Zider – cider

Shutterstock/Pincasso

Pronunciation and usage

Bristol – *Bristle*, *Brizzle* or *Brissl* as it is pronounced by the locals – is a West Country port city on the River Avon with a short length of coastline on the Severn Estuary. The local dialect, known as Bristolian, is warm in tone and lazy and rhythmic in pronunciation. Vowels are lengthened and harsh consonants are often dropped or substituted with softer ones, and the rising intonation with words added at the ends of sentences lends a gently quizzical tone to the speech of the locals. *Like, look, see* and *mind* are words which are commonly appended to the ends of sentences, for general emphasis, to ask for agreement from the listener, or to draw attention. Like is also used in the middle of sentences, perhaps to allow the speaker some thinking time – as a substitution for *ah* or *erm*.

One of the oddities of Bristol pronunciation is the *Bristol L*, which is often heard at the end of words ending in A or O, accompanied by a drawing out of the vowel sound – so that *area* becomes *areawl*, *cereal* becomes *cereawl* and *idea* becomes *ideawl*. This is a very old tendency, although opinion is divided as to whether the L is actually pronounced or whether it is merely suggested by the extended vowel sound. However, tradition suggests that the name Bristol itself comes from a contraction of the early English words *bridge* and *stowe* (or place) – *Brycgstow* or *Brigstowe*, "place by the bridge" – which over the years and with the addition of the L become *Brigstawl*, eventually contracting and arriving at Bristol. Other place names are affected – *Australiawl*, *Americawl* and *Canadawl* to name but three – and locals might have a *tunawl* sandwich for their lunch, followed by a *bananawl*, all bought from the local branch of *Asdawl* and eaten while sitting on a chair bought from *Ikeawl*.

Bristolian is known for the fact that *he* is often used to refer to impersonal objects, rather than the more usual *the* or *it*. A Bristol local who owns a small Ford car might describe it by saying *ee's a Fiestawl*. Another ancient feature is the addition of S to verbs in the first and third person. If *he goes* in Bristol, so *I goes* and *they goes*. As with other West Country dialects, including Somerset, H is often dropped from the start of words (*he* becomes *ee*, *home* becomes *ohm*), TH may become F (*teeth* become *teef*, *thanks* become *fanks*) and the suffix ING becomes EN (*runnen, jumpen, walken*). I is often used in place of me – *give it to me* becomes *give I it* – and the ER sound is emphasised and rolled when it occurs at the ends of words such as *nevER*, *clovER* and *hovER*. Where a T sound occurs in the centre of words it is generally softened or left out entirely – hence *Brissl* – and H is almost always dropped from the start of words (the same sometimes occurs with W).

A Georgian crescent in Clifton
Shutterstock/pjhpix

In common with other West Country speech patterns (and indeed with East Anglian dialects), speakers of the Bristol dialect have struggled to throw of the stigma of being yokels, rustics and somehow less civilised or intelligent than speakers of RP English. The *oooh, arrr* stereotype of the native Bristolian speaker and the lengthened sing-song sentences have clearly contributed to this, as has increased social mobility and media coverage – but Bristolians have also benefited more than other local dialect speakers, since they are perceived as more trustworthy than Cockney or Scouse speakers, for example.

Native Bristolian speakers are well known for being able to confuse non-natives with their long strings of vowel sounds, their apparent confusion between he, it, me and my, and their use of double negatives. Consider the following:

> *It allus were my waay not ta say nothing when I ant got nothing not to say.*

In the mouth of a Bristolian, this boils down to *I usually keep my mouth shut*, but an analysis of the multiple negatives might keep language scholars busy for some time. One of the other confusions of Bristolian is the verb *to be*. In the present tense, it goes *I be, thee beest, he/she/it be, we'm, you'm, they'm*. The past tense is slightly more confusing *I were, thee wer, he/she/it wer, we was, you was, they was.* The questioning future tense goes *wool I? woot? woolah? woolus? woollay? woollum?* And so on.

Other characteristic phrases include *that ain't right*, uttered at the end of a sentence to express disbelief or request clarification *(I erd you got the sack, that ain't right??)*, and *don't tell I, tell ee!* (roughly translated: that's clearly nothing to do with me, please address your enquiry to my colleague over there). The following rhyming couplet expresses disbelief that a conversational partner is not able to speak as well as they might:

Thee casn't speak as well as thee cust, cans't?

Cus if thee cuud, thee wud, usn't?

(You can't speak as well as you could, can you? Because if you could, you would, wouldn't you?)

Finally, picture the scene: two elderly ladies are standing at a bus stop; the bus is late.

Lady 1: *Fortify mince we bin stand near. Chews terbee bad, butts pasta joke now.*

Lady 2: *Feud dunce eye sedden walk tome, weed bin thereby now.*

("Forty-five minutes we've been standing here. It used to be bad, but it's past a joke now." "If you had done as I said and walked home, we would have been there by now.")

The entrance to Bristol's Exchange Market.

History, traditions and customs

The town of *Brycgstow* ("place by the bridge") was certainly in existence somewhere around 1000 AD as a Saxon market town and port, although there is evidence of earlier Paleolithic, Iron Age, Roman and early Saxon activity in the area. It was probably one of the earliest permanent bridging points of the Avon, providing communication between the two ancient kingdoms of Mercia and Wessex and later between the counties of Gloucestershire and Somerset. A motte and bailey castle and city walls were built by Geoffrey of Coutances soon after the Norman conquest in 1066, and the settlement obtained its royal charter in 1155.

It is situated on a raised tongue of land between the Rivers Avon and Frome, a site with impressive natural defences which were improved with city walls to guard the landward side of the city. Throughout the Norman era the town provided an ideal base from which to venture into south and west Wales, subduing and conquering the inhabitants. The suburb of Redcliffe on the southern bank of the Avon was subsumed into Bristol in 1373, which created a unique problem – the settlement was now in two counties, Somerset and Gloucestershire. The problem was solved in a unique way when Bristol received a charter from Edward

III which turned the town into a county in its own right.

Bristol became a busy port, ranking among the most important cities in England during the Middle Ages, along with London, York and Norwich. It was the point of embarkation for many important voyages of trade and exploration. John Cabot's voyage of discovery to Newfoundland left Bristol in 1497, financed by the local Society of Merchant Venturers and sponsored by Henry VII, and the town is thought to have received city status in 1542 during the Reformation. The city changed hands numerous times during the English Civil War, initially declaring for the Parliamentarians but falling to Prince Rupert's Royalist forces in 1643. After Royalist defeats at Langport and Bridgewater in 1645 the city also fell, despite a spirited defence by Prince Rupert's troops, and Oliver Cromwell ordered the destruction of Bristol Castle in 1656.

The city's merchants grew rich on trade with the new American colonies, but unfortunately they also invested heavily in the slave trade. Bristol had a long history of trading in people; the Normans reported that the Anglo-Saxon inhabitants of the town had grown used to trading in captured Britons and Celts, shipping them to Ireland to be sold in Dublin and other Viking ports and transported onward to labour in Iceland, Scandinavia and even Arabic

Spain. Wulfstan, the last Saxon Bishop of Worcester who was in office from 1062 to his death in 1095, was appalled by what he saw in Bristol:

They used to buy men from England and carry them to Ireland in the hope of gain; you might well groan to see the long rows of young men and maidens whose beauty might move the pity of a savage, bound together with cords and brought to market to be sold.

Wulfstan was so horrified that he worked on the stiff-necked Bristolians long and hard, staying nearby for months on end and preaching in the town's churches:

Each Sunday he would come to Bristol, and by his preaching sow the good seed, which in due time sprang up and bore fruit, so that not only did they forsake their sins, but were an example to all England.

Eventually William the Conqueror banned the slave trade in 1102, but Bristol's Norse-Irish traders were loath to give up their lucrative business; even some decades later they were infamous for inviting unsuspecting people aboard to tour or be entertained on their ships in Bristol harbour, at which point they would suddenly take sail and run for Ireland, selling their unwilling guests when they got there. Centuries later the trade revived, with manufactured goods from Bristol's industries being shipped to Africa. There the cargoes were exchanged for people, who were transported to the West Indian and American plantations.

The remains of Bristol Castle.
iStock

Finally the ships returned to Bristol laden with rum, sugar, tobacco and cocoa. The Industrial Revolution in the local area was accelerated by the demand for cheap brass goods to send to Africa, and as with other west coast port cities, notably Liverpool, this transatlantic trade triangle fuelled the development of related industries locally – cigarette making, sugar refining, and chocolate and sweet manufacture. However, the anti-slavery movement gathered pace in Bristol under the influence of locals such as William Burke, William Wordsworth and Samuel Coleridge, and the movement went on to achieve reform and also campaign for women's emancipation.

The diarist Samuel Pepys visited Bristol in 1668, and found it *in every respect another London*. A clerk to the Navy Board, Pepys was particularly keen to view the docks and quayside, and reported that it was *a most large and noble place*. By the early nineteenth century, however, the newly developed steam ships had outgrown Bristol's available anchorage; strong tides regularly left ships half buried in mud, so a section of the River Avon was enclosed to provide a new deep water pool – the Floating Harbour. Even so, it was soon impossible for the massive steamships to navigate up the river and new facilities were built downstream at Avonmouth.

Hand in hand with maritime trade went the practice of smuggling, and the Bristol Channel saw its share of contraband goods. Officials in Bristol were bribed, goods were brought ashore in smaller and less secure areas, and the illicit trade grew to become an essential part of the city's economy during the later Middle Ages.

Another important driver of the city's prosperity was the hot spring which rose through the river mud in the area of Hotwells; this brought well-off visitors from all over the country to partake of the waters which were renowned for their healing properties. There were once two pumprooms in Hotwells which catered to invalids suffering from a range of disorders, including tuberculosis. However, the spas were difficult to access – the paths to them were a *rocky and steep-winding and craggy way, near two hundred slippery steps* – and this, as well as the fact that the waters were later found to be polluted, contributed to the industry's demise in the second half of the nineteenth century.

The Floating Harbour, c1895

Street art painted as part of Bristol's See No Evil permanent
exhibition in 2011. Shutterstock/pjhpix

One of the more recent Bristol traditions is the proliferation
of street art, due in part to the success of the local artist
known as Banksy who began as a freehand graffiti artist
in Bristol in the early 1990s. He is more famous for his
stencilled works, notably *The Grim Reaper*, on the side of a
boat moored in Bristol harbour, and *Mild Mild West* in Stokes
Croft. Bristol has mostly embraced the street art culture,
celebrating it in permanent projects such as the See No Evil
installation which has transformed the formerly nondescript
Nelson Street in Bristol city centre into a riot of colour and
murals in a huge variety of styles.

Banksy's Grim Reaper, originally painted on the side of the
Thekla social boat moored in Bristol Creative Commons

51

Children, families and the church

A game once played by the children of Bristol was known as *lure*. Details of the game's rules are sketchy, but it was known to involve a group of children forming a circle and enclosing two other children inside it. When children got home from a strenuous day playing lure, the family tea may well have consisted of *pikelets*, which corresponded to modern crumpets; this word is found across the Midlands and into northern England, but it was certainly *the only word in Bristol for crumpets*.

Bristol was known for its churches and priories, with several abbeys and priories in the city during the Middle Ages, as well as hospitals run by the friars and even a leper colony outside the city walls. In the seventeenth century Bristol comprised seventeen parishes, each with its own parish church; some of these had belonged to the old abbeys or priories and became parish churches during the Reformation. Bristol's two cathedrals are active and vibrant, and the city is also home to the New Room, the oldest Methodist chapel in the world, built and used by John Wesley and still complete with the rooms above the chapel itself where Wesley and other prominent Methodists stayed while they preached to Bristol's poor.

The poor themselves were well catered for, with the Bristol Corporation of the Poor formed in 1696 to operate a poor relief system across the city. Buildings were built or rented to act as workhouses, with the initial establishment set up in 1698 to cater for a hundred pauper girls. They were taught to read (although not to write) and employed to cook and wash, spin and weave. A workhouse for the elderly, boys and young children followed in 1699, with inmates being taught to spin and weave, and the elderly being *given such Employments as were fit for their Ages and Strengths*.

However, the workhouses were not pleasant places to live and work. Illnesses were common, and in 1711 an anonymous critic claimed the Bristol workhouses were *crowded with idle, Lazy and Lewd people*. Later reports suggested that the houses were *infested with vermin*, and criminals and other social undesirables had joined the genuinely destitute: *vagrants are kept separate from regular inmates. Prostitutes wear a yellow dress and single pregnant women wear a red dress; they are kept separate from the rest and not allowed to associate with the children*.

Bristol Cathedral and its environs

From the middle of the nineteenth century children in particular were very well cared for in Bristol through the work of George Müller, a Prussian immigrant who was so affected by the plight of the poor that he and his wife began to take orphans into their own home, and eventually he built the orphanages at Ashley Down. He only ever accepted unsolicited gifts for his work, never going into debt and sometimes being saved from hunger or penury by the most miraculous-seeming events. Once the children and orphanage staff sat down at table to give thanks to God for their breakfast, even though there was no food in the house, and just as they finished praying a baker knocked at the door with enough bread to feed them all, and a milkman's cart broke down just outside the gate so he donated all his fresh milk.

Bristol is home to a number of professional sports teams, notably Bristol City Football Club who play in the English Football League, and the city is also the headquarters of Gloucestershire County Cricket Club. Bristol City FC was founded in 1897 when the amateur Bristol South End club turned professional, joining the Football League in 1901. The Club's nickname is *The Robins* and they play at the Ashton Gate stadium. They are one of a select number of English clubs who have won the Welsh Cup, beating

Tranmere Rovers to take the title in 1934. Like most football clubs Bristol City are famous for having their own chants, many aimed at their traditional rivals Bristol Rovers, a non-league club founded in 1883 and originally known as Eastville Rovers:

Drink up thy cider, drink up thy cider,
For tonight we merry be;
We're going down the Rovers to take the Eastville over,
And there's still more cider in the jar!

Bristol Rovers' nickname is *The Gas*, from the gasworks next to their former home at Eastville before their move to the Memorial Stadium at Horfield. The two clubs contest the Bristol derby, each viewing the other as their traditional rivals, and there is often a heated atmosphere:

Hark now hear the City sing,
And Rovers ran away;
And we will sing forever more,
Because of derby day!

Industry and agriculture

Industries in Bristol have included tobacco, chocolate, aircraft, glass, paper, soap, chemicals, wine and sherry, with the famous Bristol Cream sherry a legacy of the city's heritage importing spirits and fortified wines from Spain and beyond. The growth of some industries was the consequence of incoming trade from Europe and beyond, while others were assisted by Bristol's status as the terminus of Isambard Kingdom Brunel's Great Western Railway. In more recent times the city has become an important financial centre and high technology hub.

The city also has a reputation for major engineering works – not least the Floating Harbour on the Avon, but also the Clifton Suspension Bridge, designed by Brunel to span the Avon gorge and give enough clearance for tall ships to pass beneath on their way upriver to the Floating Harbour. Brunel was convalescing in Bristol after an accident involving a tunnel collapse in Rotherhithe, and he won a competition with his bridge design, but only after persuading the judging panel of the merits of his ideas and going against the advice of his father, Marc Isambard Brunel, who did not believe that the bridge would be stable without a central pillar. After encountering construction and funding difficulties during Brunel's lifetime the bridge was eventually completed in 1864, five years after his death. He had described it *as my first child, my darling*, and it is fitting that it stands as his memorial.

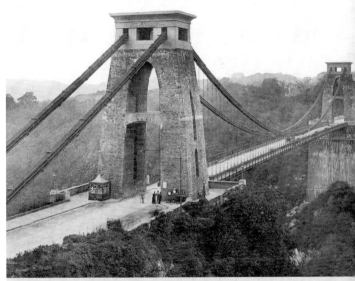

The Clifton Suspension Bridge, c1900
www.pastandpresentpublications.com

The bridge is seventy-five metres above the river and has a reputation for suicides, but not all who fell from the bridge were killed. Two children, Ruby and Elsie Brown, were thrown from the bridge by their deranged father on a stormy night in 1896 but they survived, cushioned by gusts of wind and plunging into the river only feet from a passing pilot boat which rescued them in short order. However, the most famous survivor was Sarah Ann Henley, a twenty-two-year-old barmaid who jumped from the bridge when she was jilted by her lover. Local tradition states that she was saved from the river by an updraft of air which caught in her skirt and created a parachute effect, directing her to land in the thick mud on the Gloucestershire bank of the river, instead of in the water. She was rescued by passers-by and a local GP and taken to hospital, although initially a cab driver refused to transport her there because she was too muddy (in response to pleas from the doctor that she would die without swift transport, the driver is reported to have said, *"I don't care. Let her die"*). Stretcher bearers were eventually summoned from the local police station and she arrived at the hospital an hour later.

A verse by William Heasell commemorates the miraculous event:

Once in Victoria's golden age
When crinolines were all the rage,
A dame in fashionable attire
Would change her life for one up higher.
So up to Clifton Bridge she went
And made a parachute descent;

But though 'twas not the lady's wish,
A boatman hooked her like a fish,
And thus a slave to fashion's laws
Was snatched from out of Death's hungry jaws.
This story's true, I'd have you know,
And thus it only goes to show.

In fact, Sarah Ann went on to make a full recovery. While she was in hospital recovering from internal injuries sustained in her fall she received several proposals of marriage. She did not accept any of them, but she did go on to marry some years later; she eventually died in 1948 aged eighty-five, and is buried in the Avonview Cemetery, some way upstream of her abortive attempted suicide.

As well as trade from the sea, Bristol was a centre for agricultural trading from the surrounding countryside in Somerset, Gloucestershire and Wiltshire. Labourers in the local fields would cease their work to have their *nummet*, a plain meal without meat usually eaten either mid-morning or mid-afternoon during a pause from their labours. (It was sometimes said that local labourers had seven meals a day, of which nummet was one.)

The Avon gorge and the suspension bridge, showing the mudflats which saved Sarah Ann's life www.pastandpresentpublications.com

Farmers would bring their wares to market on *draws* or *gehoes*, which were sledge-type affairs without wheels that were pulled by horses. Tradition has it that these wheel-less vehicles were preferred to the more usual wheeled carts because of the fact that Bristol contains many *goutes*, or underground passages built to carry watercourses, and there were fears that the rumbling of cart wheels on the cobbled streets above might dislodge stones from the tunnels below. On their way to the city the gehoes would struggle to travel over ruts in the roads, and farmers were known to send loads of *nickies* (bundles of thorns or hedge-clippings) on ahead with an extra labourer, whose job it was to fill the worst of the ruts so that the gehoes could be pulled more easily.

The Avon, the Severn and the sea

Bristol grew up on the banks of the Rivers Avon and Frome, and since the thirteenth century its waterways have been modified to act as docks. The River Avon empties into the River Severn, which is renowned for its high tides; as a consequence the Avon also has tides which fluctuate by about nine metres between high and low water, which in turn means that the river is easily navigable at high tide but is a muddy channel at low tide. Ships would often run aground and be stranded on the mud at low tide, leading to the phrase *ship shape and Bristol fashion*, meaning tidily stowed and secured and describing ships that were securely loaded and capable of taking the strain of repeated groundings.

Bristol was an embarkation point for explorers and traders down the centuries, with sailors travelling regularly to Iceland from as early as the fifteenth century. Many famous mariners left from Bristol – John Cabot's voyage aboard the *Matthew* to discover Newfoundland was only one of these – but it is a lesser known fact that a Bristol native was involved in the real-life story that inspired Daniel Defoe to write the tale of *Robinson Crusoe*. Woodes Rogers was a captain and privateer who grew up in and around Bristol, finding himself in control of his family's shipping business at the age of only twenty-seven. He led a privateering expedition against the Spanish from 1708 to 1711, circumnavigating the globe and capturing several Spanish vessels. On the way, in February 1709 he also rescued Alexander Selkirk, another privateer, who had been marooned on the uninhabited archipelago of Juan Fernández off the coast of Chile for over four years.

Unlike Crusoe, Selkirk was not shipwrecked; he had asked to be put ashore in September 1704 because of grave concerns about the seaworthiness of the *Cinque Ports*, an English galley also engaged in buccaneering operations

The statue commemorating the voyage of John Cabot from Bristol in June 1497. He made landfall probably at Cape Bonavista in Newfoundland, and is widely believed to be the first European to set foot in America since the Vikings

The inscription on the side of the statue

against the Spanish. (He was right to be concerned; the *Cinque Ports* later sank off Colombia.) Selkirk survived by hunting, fishing, utilising the island's natural resources and domesticating feral cats to protect him from attack by rats.

He became a celebrity on his return to Britain with Captain Rogers, but soon returned to sea, dying of yellow fever in 1721 while on an anti-piracy patrol off West Africa. Rogers himself was twice appointed the colonial Governor of the Bahamas, where he cleansed the colony of pirates, warded off the Spanish and established commerce.

Meanwhile, trade in Bristol grew steadily; tobacco formed a major proportion of the tonnage passing through the city, but wine, olive oil, iron, dried fruits and dyes also arrived from Europe and beyond, while cloth, lead, ore and hides formed major exports. Certain Bristol trading terms have remained in the language down the years. The phrase *to pay for something on the nail* is thought to stem from Bristol traders and merchants, who used to buy and sell by the four bronze pillars in front of the Exchange building. These pillars were known as the Nails, hence the expression – pay for it on the nail. The Avonmouth dockers who loaded and unloaded all the cargoes down the 'Mouth were a breed apart, welcoming the work even though it was often low paid and back-breaking. They had to haul loads of a hundred pounds or more on their backs up and down gangplanks (known as *shivers)* which had no guard rails, although surprisingly few of them fell in the water. Some cargoes carried special rates – dockers got a shilling a day *splinter money* for unloading timber, sixpence a day *sticky money* for sugar, and fourpence a day for ochre.

Shipbuilding at Bristol was a vibrant industry, but it too was hampered by the high tidal surges. There were a number of shipping disasters in the Avon Gorge; the worst of these was the *Demerara* in 1851. She had been built at Patterson's Shipyard and was being manoeuvred by tugs down the gorge on her maiden voyage when the tide turned. She lurched out of control and became stuck on rocks, remaining lodged there until the next high tide. She then refloated, drifted out of control again and became wedged across the river, blocking all shipping. The Great Western shipping company was formed in 1835 to run a trans-Atlantic passenger route, and indeed the company's first steamer, the *Great Western*, was a success. However, the *Great Western* alone was unable to make the route profitable, and the Cunard company in Liverpool had soon built four ships and begun to take the passenger trade away from Bristol. The Great Western company responded by building the massive iron *Great Britain*, but she proved to be too large to pass through the docks on her way down the Avon and her launch was delayed. She eventually made a few successful voyages, but then ran aground on the northeast coast of Ireland and was eventually converted into a sailing ship. After a chequered career she ended up as a storage hulk in Port Stanley in the Falklands, but she has now been returned to Bristol and restored; she is in the dry dock where she was built, forming one of the area's finest visitor attractions.

Smuggling was a major occupation in Bristol, with the city's traders both importing and exporting a variety of illicit goods. During the Spanish Armada in the sixteenth century there was a roaring trade in culverin guns and ammunition, made in the Forest of Dean and smuggled abroad via Bristol for sale to the Spanish; the Armada was quite literally armed by the country it was aimed at. Wine from France and the Mediterranean was brought ashore during Tudor times, with customs officers pocketing large bribes to charge duty on only a fraction of the cargoes unloading on the dockside. Tobacco took over as the major illicit import in the seventeenth and eighteenth centuries; ships' masters routinely kept two sets of books, one correct and the other for the customs authorities, to be handed over with a hefty bribe. Indeed, studies of commercial records suggest that smuggling was a significant part of Bristol's business over a number of centuries, with many of the city's elite engaging in it, often working closely with corrupt customs officials.

The SS Great Britain, c1904 www.pastandpresentpublications.com

Hand in hand with trade and smuggling went piracy, and some of the most notorious pirates every to haunt the Spanish Main hailed from Bristol. One of the most famous of these was Edward Teach, better known as Blackbeard, who was probably born in Redcliff and whose reign of terror claimed many lives. He was described as a large strong man with a huge black beard, which he wore braided and sometimes stuck full of lighted matches or fuses during attacks on other ships to create an image of *such a figure that imagination cannot form an idea of a fury from hell to look more frightful.*

However, contrary to his fearsome depictions in film and literature he commanded his vessels with the permission of their crews, relying on his terrifying personal appearance and reputation to do much of his work for him, and there is no evidence that he harmed or threatened those he took hostage. Legend has it that during his final battle off North Carolina on 22 November 1718 he sustained five gunshot wounds and more than twenty sword cuts, but when his apparently dead body was thrown overboard he still swam three times around his ship, the *Adventure*, before finally giving up the ghost.

Edward Teach, more commonly known as Blackbeard –
a native of Bristol Creative Commons

Nevertheless, perhaps Bristol's most enduring piratical legacy is pirate-speak, the stereotypical *oooh, arrr, me hearties* dialect which has been presented by Hollywood in many films. While it is true that many Bristol mariners (such as Blackbeard himself) did turn to piracy, our notions of their speech stem probably from the movie portrayals of Long John Silver and Blackbeard given by Robert Newton, himself a native of the West Country who emphasised his accent for the roles. The archetypal pirate exclamations of *arrr!* or *yarr!* could have been heard on any Bristol street corner, but Robert Newton made them famous, for which he has been made the 'patron saint' of International Talk Like A Pirate Day, which takes place on September 19 every year.

Last word

The last word in this book must go to a poet known as Agrikler, who recorded a good deal of Bristol and West Country dialect in a series of poems originally published in the Bristol Times and Mirror towards the end of the nineteenth century. The poems dealt with local West Country matters such as country fairs, local news stories and personages, but they also encompassed wider issues and stories with morals attached that were suitable for a larger circle of readers. Gathered together, the rhymes were eventually published under the general heading of *Agrikler's Proverbeel Feelossify*. One of his rhymes exemplifies the laid-back West Country way of life, beginning thus:

When thengs goo ta rack and ruin,
Thaw you'm nither sick ner lazy,
Ther's a maxim wuth the doin –
Take et yazy.

Hard work – nothin's done athout it –
Ef ye got ta much ta plaze ye,
Taint no use ta swear about it –
Take et yazy.

Thaw ye mid be in a hurry,
Thaw a thousand duties chaze ye –
Nothin's done by fuss and flurry –
Take et yazy.

Bristol waterfront Shutterstock/Matt Gore

Bibliography

A number of writers have celebrated and preserved the Bristol dialect, and as a consequence there is a variety of resources available. There is a broad range of modern material, written by enthusiastic and knowledgeable folk, but I have tried to go as far back as possible to track down antiquarian sources who experienced and recorded the ancient dialect as it was spoken tens or even hundreds of years ago, or to attested literary works which record the local vernacular in the dialogue of the characters. Among the most useful resources have been the following:

Edwards, Joseph: *Rhymes in the West of England Dialect, by Agrickler*. Leech and Taylor, 1872.

Jones, Evan: *Inside the Illicit Economy: Reconstructing the smugglers' trade of sixteenth century Bristol*. Ashgate, 2011.

Robinson, Derek and Wiltshire, Vic: *A Load of Old Bristle: Krek Waiter's Peak Bristle*. Newbury, Berkshire: Countryside Books, 2002.

Robinson, Derek and Wiltshire, Vic: *Sick Sentries of Bristle. Newbury, Berkshire:* Countryside Books, 2004.

Smith, Lucy Toulmin (Ed.): *The Maire of Bristowe, Is Kalendar by Robert Ricart, 1472*. The Camden Society, 1872.

Stoke, Harry and Green, Vinny: *A Dictionary of Bristle*. Bristol: Tangent Books, 2012.

Wright, Joseph: *The English Dialect Dictionary.* Oxford University Press, 1889–1905.

There is also a rich diversity of online resources, which have been collected and collated by many dedicated individuals. Among the most interesting are:

The BBC Voices project: http://www.bbc.co.uk/voices/

Another BBC guide to Bristolian phrases: http://www.bbc.co.uk/bristol/content/madeinbristol/culture/b.shtml

A useful history of Bristol at the Building History page: http://www.buildinghistory.org/bristol/

Bristol Past: http://www.bristolpast.co.uk/

Online Bristolian dictionaries at: http://www.mintinit.com/speakbristolian.php and http://www.thedialectdictionary.com/view/letter/Bristol/